"If God Is EVERYWHERE,
He is in your underwear"
*
FIRST INSIGHTS
Of a Child

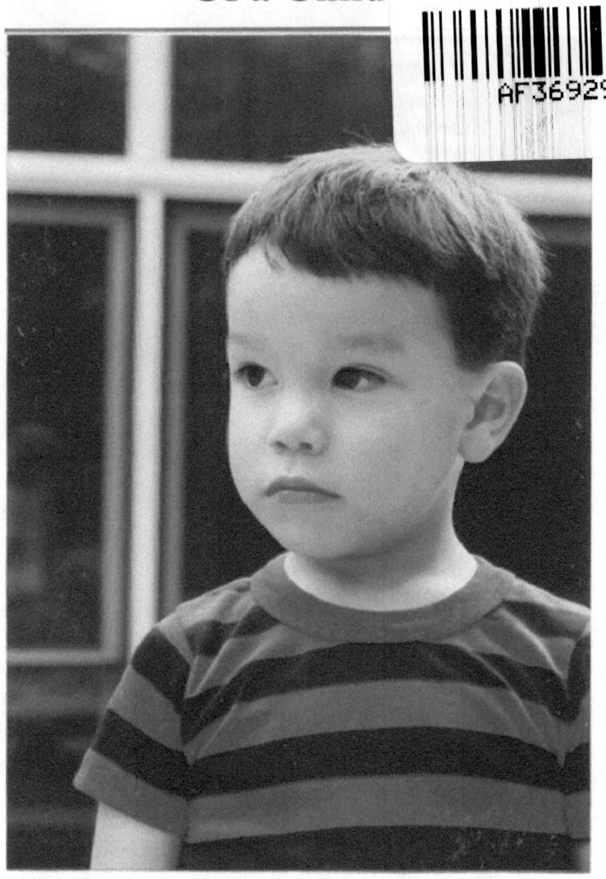

compiled by his father
Richard Weekley

Cyberwit.net
HIG 45 Kaushambi Kunj, Kalindipuram
Allahabad - 211011 (U.P.) India
http://www.cyberwit.net
Tel: +(91) 9415091004
E-mail: info@cyberwit.net

Printed at Thomson Press India Limited.

"Dad I got a poem"

<u>Introductory Stuff</u>

Becoming a first time parent at 42 was my ultimate terror (because I knew nothing) and a supreme delight. I'd never raised a tiny human creature so I had no idea what to do. My wife Rosalba who previously raised her daughter Patty helped immensely, but I was terrified I'd blow it! But at the same time, I was absolutely exultant at experiencing this marvelous gift of nature –John Matthew Weekley.

Being a writer/poet, I could not stop myself from catching the FOUND POEMS that slipped from his lips as his mind began to connect the dots of his world. He spoke candid words born from complete innocence.

Now, years later, I'm looking back and marveling what was phrases were netted.

I hope no one forgets don't forget my son, Matthew's philosophical observation at age 5, *"If God is everywhere, he is in your underwear."*

Richard Weekley

My son, John Matthew Weekley, reading a poem at a poetic
Halloween gathering.
Age 12

*"If God Is Everywhere,
He Is in
Your Underwear"*

*

FIRST

INSIGHTS

Of a Child

Compiled by

Richard Weekley

CONTENTS

Adults know everything Don't they Dad?

Matthew Lage, says so*

*A Childhood friend

When is it tomorrow?

(Matt was puzzled because 'tomorrow' never arrived.)

I want to make the rules

There's not a single thing to do

You want to hear
some good news
before
its bad news??

When you get older
you can stay up
as late as you want

A blessing composed before a meal.
Note: Matt had a devoted Evangelical Grandmother
and a Buddhist father.

Dear Jesus,

Thank you for Buddha

"If God Is Everywhere, He Is in Your Underwear"

I guess

I'm not shy

anymore

I'm getting used
to the socks.

I want to do something

There's nothing I want to do

I wish I was a baby again

The moon – was born?

How do you get
a girl friend?

I LOVE WORDS

Age 6

Once more Dad - -

just once more

If playing tether ball or catch with me

What's an ex-wife?

I have this feeling
I can't explain

I don't want to be here
And I don't want to go

I know who
The tooth-fairy is

Age 6

Christmas eve.
Santa Clause arrived
at the door
with presents

After a few minutes
Matt jumped up
and pulled on
Santa's beard
and
discovered his sister.

age 6

Daddy, another thing

**You can't hug when you're
in the Marines?**

**You can't feel
what another person feels**

**Because
You're not that person**

Right?

**I try to remember
if I felt something like that...**

**I want to feel
how people feel**

Age 6

I have this feeling inside

**I want to do
two things at the same time**

**Dad, did you know
you have a gray hair growing
in your ear?**

Did you huh?

Dad
can I have the house
when you die?

What's a scare-dee-cat?

There's nothing to be afraid of
There's nothing to be afraid of
There s nothing to be afraid of

Age 6

Matt kept repeating
these word as he played
tether ball into
November darkness.

(Looking in the mirror)

I don't look the same as I used to

\-

I'm changing

Everybody does
different things
in
their houses - - -

right?

When I'm 18

will my bed time still be

9 o'clock?

I wish I was 12

Age 7

You know why
I wanted a Walkman?

Cause
I saw it on TV
and
it makes me look older

Age 7

I know where heaven is - -

It's in the earth

age 7

[My Life at 7]*

Actually untitled writing by Matt

I can spell Matthew Lage   [a playmate]
and I can tell you more
yes patty [his big sister] goes a to the Boys and Girls Club.
And Tippy [his small dog] sits in the shade all day.
and Daddy bought a new car.

and I passed the swim test.
and we're going swimming today.
my dad won a tennis trophy.
when my dad was little he had no TV.
and when my dad was little he got hit in the head
with a shovel and lived on a peach ranch.

and our neighbors drew pictures on the wall.
my friend Ernesto keeps wanting to borrow video games.
I take a walk every day.
my dad meditates every day and exercises.
And Tippy eats grass every day.
we grow grapes.
my dad types almost every day.

[Recalling a trip to Sea World]
I went bungee jumping.
I found a rainbow fish
and I saw a shark - it was a hammerhead.
I saw other sharks too.
and a whale splashed us with its tail.
And we saw the dolphin show.
And after that we had lunch and I had spaghetti.

And my dad won a skiing trophy.
And my sister slept in until10:00
Patty loves the Olsen Twins.
And "It Takes Two."

And my dad doesn't play video games.
And my dad plays baseball and tickles me.
My dad is a great driver.
When my dad was little he got
hit in the head by the car door.

[Next stanza is about our beach house in Rosarito, Baja California]

And tippy sits in his hole all day.
and we go to the beach every day
and take a run to Rosarito Beach Hotel.
and tippy keep's digging holes all day
and wrestles my dad.

and I climbed the pole.
and we go to Jack in the Box for lunch.
and I do flips on the bed and twist in the air
and bounced on the bed
and jump.

Mommy eats too many tacos.
and Tippy barks at other dogs.
and Patty wears a green mask.
and mommy takes wilds pictures.

(Form and spelling modified for easier reading)

I think the door
Was made in China

China
makes everything

Age 8

Dad

What's a pervert?

Age 8

How come people don't want weeds in their yards?

Age 8

I explained reproduction to Matt.
Later he asked

Daddy
How do I get it out?

Age 8

(Matt began playing baseball at age 6)

I'm not afraid

but
my legs shake
when I' m up to bat

Why?

Age 8

I scolded Matt
for playing a violent video game
-Road Rash-

You're getting old

and your brain

is getting smaller

Age 8

Dad

Did great –
Almost hit it over

But can you
feed the pets?

age 9

Look Dad!

All the notes
start going around
in my mind

And my fingers know
where they are going
without looking

Age 9

I wish

they didn't have grades

they make me feel bad

Age 9

Dad this is my last time
Dad this is my *very* last time
Dad this is my *very, very* last time

Dad this is my *very, very, very* last time

I swear

Really Dad, this is it

Age 9

**Children learn by imitating
the sounds and behaviors
around them.**

I was amazing by some of Matt's

FIRST POEMS

*They are typed and re-aligned
from Matt's penciled scrawl.*

Buddha Tells Me

Buddha tells me that

the sea is my teacher

the rocks are the birds

I thought I never hear that

I never understood

But the sea taught me

all I had to know

He taught me sun, creature, and animal

That's when the sea touched me.

age 8

The Sea Lives

Buddha tells me that

the sea is alive

But I thought

it was dead

The sea told me

look in your heart

and the sea sang a song I never understood

until *now*

--My Dad told me what it meant

age 8

The Sun Is

The sun is   the fire

the fire   is the sun

The sun is   the Buddha

That lives inside all of us

Age 8

Buddha Is Powerful

Buddha is powerful

Because the sun becomes him

and *the wind becomes all living creatures.*

age 8

Wild Sounds

The birds make sounds

The frogs make sounds

And other sounds you *cannot hear*

Like dogs barking

flowers

and

Buddha.

age 8

THE FLOWER
is the sun

The sun is the birds

the birds are that song
that lives inside all of us

age 8

THE SUN CAN SING
But cannot sleep

The moon can sing
But cannot talk

You need light
The green light you cannot see
unless
you have the flower

The flower that brings
enlightenment

I call this love
that I can bring to you

Age 9

WHAT IF

There was no WHAT IF?

WHAT IF...

WHAT IF...

WHAT IF...

DOGS MEOWING

Sun darkening
Purple sky
Black grass

I think I'm going crazy
but
you never know
when
you're having fun

The sky is blue and has a life
but
What am I
and the sea
and the trees?

Or am I the clouds
or sun
who knows
what I could be?

But I am glad
for what I am

Age 10

I LIVE IN

**a world
of plastic fires**

**and electric
make believe color**

ZEN OUR TEACHER

teaches us how
to live without
pain and suffering

but to respect
animals for what
they are

and to respect
others for what
they are going
to be

now Zen
our teacher is
our future of
enlightenment
and joy.

Read at the mic by Matt 4/25/99 at the publication of Vol No.'s "Overload" issue.

Age 10

ON A WINTER NIGHT SKY

The moon rises

On a winter night sky
the wind blows
leaves off chairs

And on a winter night sky
a poem rises

On a winter night sky
the full moon cries
while the wind
blows nature away

and on a winter sky
a poem is written

On a winter night sky
the moon cries over
the dreadful days
that it has lived

And while the full moon cries
its sorrow
a new day comes
looking for a good poem
to write.

Age 11

Right now I see the weaved metal
under my bed staring me down
as I lie here writing

I hear cars fly down the narrow street

I smelled the lingering taste of pastries as I
walked
by the French Bakery

I touch the green carpet
of our bedroom floor
fifty stories high

Inside I am like a bird soaring
freely through the Eifel tower

I remember the scare
of going to the top.

Paris, age 13

I am seeing mini-cars parked
along the sides of the miniscule road

I hear the whistle of the train
zooming into the station

I sense the lingering
taste of pizza

Adventure and the smells of home
await me

I touch the food on the plate
seeing if it moves
or if it is still alive

Inside I am like a traveler
on an excursion

I remember the buildings
that shined upon me
with brightness.

Paris, age 13

Epilogue

To make a long story short, in college Matthew preferred and excelled in the poetry of Mathematics over the poetry of words.

I do feel his early interactions with poetry enriched his life and mine.

I'm pleased he found a career path as a radiologic technician at Los Angeles' Cedar Sinai hospital, which pays abundantly more than poetry.

APPENDIX

Some samples of Matthew's writing as originally penned.

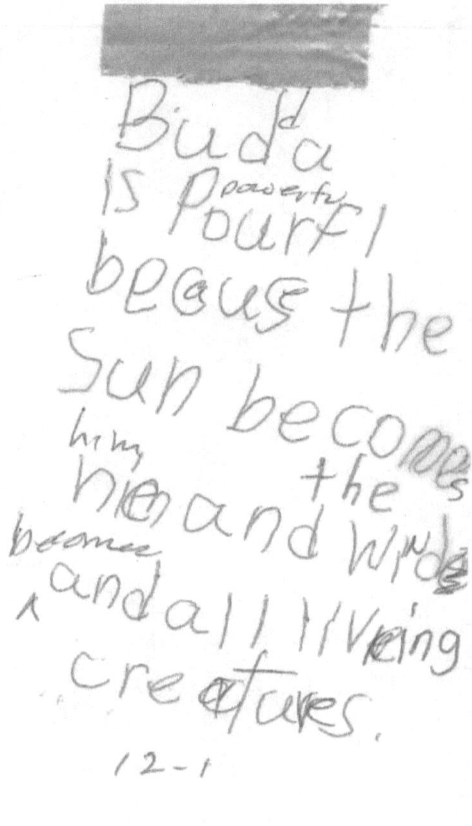

Buddha Tells Me

Buddha tells me that
the sea is my teacher
the rocks are the birds
I thought I never
hear that I never
understood but the sea
tough me all that
I had to now he
tough me sun creatur
and animal that ween
the sea touched me.

Buda tells ~~me~~

~~Budallet~~

Buda tells me that
the sea is my techer
the rocks are the
brids I thouf I nevr
hear that I nevr
under stoud
but the sea to taught
me all that
I had to now
he tot me san
crechr and anamal
that when the sea
tuch me.

the sea lives
Buda tells me that
the seais alive but
I thout it was ded
he told me look
in your hart and
he saig a sogn that
I never undrstood
intel now my dad
told me what it
ment.

On a winter nightsky the
moonrises on a winter night sky, the
wind blows leaves of charirs and on
a winter night sky a poem rises

On a winter night sky the full moon
crys ~~On a winter night sky~~ while the
wind blows nature away and on a winter
sky a poem is written

On a winter night sky the moon is
over it's dreadful days it has lived and
while the full moon crys its so proud
as new day comes learking for
a good poem to write

12-11-99

Right now I see the weaved
metal under my bed staring
me down as I lie here writing
I hear cars fly down
the narrow street
Right now I smell the
lingering taste of
pastries as I walk
by the French Bakery
The faint ~~home of~~ (smell)
of home awaits me
I touch the green
carpet of our bedroom
floor fifty stories
high
Inside I am like a
~~to you~~ bird soaring
freely through the
Eifel Tower
I remember going to the ~~force~~
the Eifel Tower scarely

6/16/02 Excerpt 02
prill.

I am seeing minicars parked along
the sides of the miniscule road
I hear the whistling of
the train ~~some going~~ zooming
into the station
I sense the lingering taste
of pizza & andventure nearby
The faint smell of Newhall
awaits me
I touch the food on the
plane seeing if it moves
or if its still alive
Inside I am ~~~~ like a trailer
on a excursion
I ~~remember~~ the buildings that
shinned apon me with
brightness

Weekley, a second-generation poet, reads some verse he composed that morning.

"...10-year old Matthew Weekley stood behind a microphone and unfolded a piece of paper.

Smiling he read one of his own creations, a short poem about Zen, which concluded "is our future of enlightenment."   [Carol Rock, reporter]